LET'S CELEBRATE WITH ORIGAMI

Let's Celebrate with More
HANUKKAH ORIGAMI

By Ruth Owen

Enslow PUBLISHING

Published in 2022 by Enslow Publishing, LLC
29 East 21st Street
New York, NY 10010

Copyright © 2022 Enslow Publishing, LLC
All rights reserved.

Produced for Rosen by Ruth Owen Books
Designer: Emma Randall
Photos courtesy of Ruth Owen Books and Shutterstock

Cataloging-in-Publication Data

Names: Owen, Ruth.
Title: Let's celebrate with more Hanukkah origami / Ruth Owen.
Description: New York : Enslow Publishing, 2022. | Series: Let's celebrate with origami |
Includes glossary and index.
Identifiers: ISBN 9781978526631 (pbk.) | ISBN 9781978526655 (library bound) |
ISBN 9781978526648 (6 pack) | ISBN 9781978526662 (ebook)
Subjects: LCSH: Origami--Juvenile literature. | Hanukkah decorations--Juvenile literature.
Classification: LCC TT870.O946 2022 | DDC 736'.982--dc23

Manufactured in the United States of America

CPSIA compliance information: Batch #CWENS22: For further information contact Enslow Publishing, New York, New York at 1-800-398-2504

Find us on

Contents

An Origami Holiday 4

Origami Tips 6

Paper Stars 8

Holiday Wreath 12

Simple Origami Menorah 16

Origami Baskets 20

A Box for Gifts...................................... 24

A Bow for Gifts..................................... 28

Glossary, Index, Websites 32

An Origami Holiday

If you've never tried **origami** before, don't worry! This book will take you step by step through six fun holiday projects.

Origami is the art of folding paper to make small **sculptures**, or models. This popular art form gets its name from the Japanese words "ori," which means folding, and "kami," which means paper. People have been making origami models in Japan for hundreds of years.

Hanukkah is all about celebrating with family and enjoying gifts, blessings, burning candles, and food. It's also the perfect time to get creative with origami by making beautiful paper Hanukkah decorations and gifts.

So grab some blue, white, and silver paper, and let's get folding!

Origami Tips

Follow these tips for successful folding and origami model making.

Tip 1
Read all the instructions carefully and look at the pictures. Make sure you understand what's required before you begin a fold. Don't rush; be patient. Work slowly and carefully.

Tip 2
Folding a piece of paper sounds easy, but it can be tricky to get neat, accurate folds. The more you practice, the easier it becomes.

Tip 3
If an instruction says "crease," make the crease as flat as possible. The flatter the creases, the better the model. You can make a sharp crease by running a plastic ruler along the edge of the paper.

Tip 4
Sometimes, at first, your models may look a little crumpled. Don't give up! The more models you make, the better you will get at folding and creasing.

When it comes to origami, practice makes perfect!

The complicated gift box and amazing paper stars on this page were made by experienced model makers. But keep practicing your folding skills and you could soon become an origami master and be ready to make difficult models like these!

When you turn the page, you'll find instructions for making paper Stars of David. You can turn your origami stars into a hanging decoration. All you need to do is use clothespins and a piece of string to create a decoration that's quick to make but has a cool vintage look.

Paper Stars

Get started on your Hanukkah holiday decorations by folding some blue and white six-pointed origami stars.

The six-pointed Star of David has been used as a **symbol** on Jewish prayer books, religious objects, and buildings for more than 1,000 years. The star has also been an **emblem** of the Jewish people.

The Star of David is usually shown in blue and white. These colors are also associated with the Jewish people. Blue and white are the colors of the tallit, the prayer shawl worn over the shoulders at Jewish Sabbath, holiday, and morning services.

To make a Star of David, you will need:

One sheet of paper that's blue, white, or silver

(Origami paper is sometimes colored on both sides or white on one side.)

STEP 1:

Begin with a piece of paper that is rectangular.

STEP 2:

Place the paper colored side down, fold in half, crease, and unfold.

STEP 3:

Now fold down the top left-hand corner so that the point touches the center crease and the bottom left-hand corner forms a sharp point. Crease well.

The top left-hand point should touch the center crease.

The bottom left-hand corner should form a point once the fold is made.

Make sure these two edges line up.

STEP 4:
Now fold down the top right-hand corner of the model so that it forms a triangle shape and the two edges of the paper line up on the left-hand side. Crease well.

Fold up the bottom right-hand point of the model along the dotted line, and tuck it inside the model.

STEP 5:
Fold down the top point of the model so it meets the base of the model, crease hard, and unfold.

Now repeat on the two side points of the model.

STEP 6:

Turn the model over. Fold down the top point of the model so the point touches the middle of the triangle in the center of the model, crease hard, and unfold.

Now repeat on the two side points of the model. Your model should now have six creases and look like this.

STEP 7:

Turn the model back over. Now using the creases you made in steps 5 and 6, create a pleat in the top point of the model. Then make a pleat with the left-hand point of the model.

Finally, make a pleat with the right-hand point of the model. Then tuck this pleat under one of the others to secure all three pleats.

Turn your star over, and it is complete!

Holiday Wreath

This Hanukkah, try making a wreath to decorate one of the doors of your home. A wreath made from origami is a modular model, which means it's made in small sections that are then slotted together.

To make your Hanukkah wreath, you can use origami paper in white and shades of blue. You can also use recycled gift-wrapping paper to add patterned effects or silver to your decoration.

Try making the basic wreath design and then decorate it with Hanukkah symbols such as the stars you made in the first project. Have fun!

To make a wreath, you will need:

8 sheets of paper in your choice of blue, white, or silver. Eight pieces of paper, each measuring 6 inches (15 cm) square, will make a wreath with a diameter of about 10 inches (25 cm).

Glue

Decorations for the wreath, such as paper Stars of David

STEP 1:
Place the paper colored side down, fold in half diagonally, and crease.

STEP 2:
Now fold up the right-hand point of the model, and crease hard.

STEP 3:
Then fold the top layer back down again along the dotted line, and crease hard.

13

STEP 4:

The right-hand point will have formed a small pocket. Gently open up the pocket and then carefully squash and flatten it back down so it forms a square.

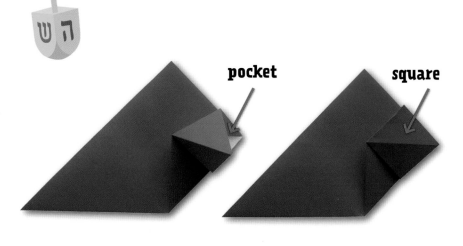

STEP 5:

Turn the model over. Fold down the top layer of paper along the dotted line, and crease.

STEP 6:

Fold in the right-hand point of the model, and crease hard.

STEP 7:

Turn the model back over, and your first module is complete. Repeat steps 1 to 6 with each of the other pieces of paper until you have eight modules in total.

STEP 8:

Now take two modules and slot them together as shown.

Turn the model over and the two modules should look like this.

Now, folding along the dotted line, fold back the point of the light blue module so it tucks under and inside the part of the dark blue module directly beneath it.

point

This fold will join the two modules, but for added security you can also tape or glue them together.

Keep joining the modules together, and finally attach module one to module eight to complete the wreath. Glue Stars of David or other decorations to your wreath.

Simple Origami Menorah

Hanukkah celebrates a **miracle** that happened more than 2,000 years ago. At that time, the Jews were ruled by the Syrian-Greeks, who tried to force the Jews to give up their religion. The Jews fought back, and won. When they went to rededicate their temple by lighting the holy lamp, there was only enough oil for one day. The oil miraculously lasted for eight days, however, until more oil arrived.

Hanukkah is also known as the Festival of Lights. Every evening during Hanukkah, Jews light candles in a menorah. A menorah holds eight candles, one for each day of the miracle, and a ninth candle called the shammash, which is used to light the others. This year, using nine tealights and your paper-folding skills, try making a simple origami menorah.

To make an origami tealight menorah, you will need:

18 squares of paper in your choice of white, silver, and shades of blue

9 tealight candles or 9 LED tealights

STEP 1:

To make each candleholder, you will need two pieces of paper in different colors. Begin by placing one sheet of paper with the color you want facing up. We chose dark blue.

Fold the paper in half from side to side, crease, and unfold. Then fold up the bottom half of the paper, and crease.

STEP 2:

Now fold the paper in half again, crease well, and then unfold.

STEP 3:

Now fold up the two bottom corners of the model so they meet the center crease, and crease hard.

STEP 4:

Now, folding only the top layer of paper, fold down the two top corners, and crease.

STEP 5:
Fold down the top flap of the model, and crease.

STEP 6:
Turn the model over, and it should look like this.

Now fold down the top two corners so they meet the center crease, and crease well.

STEP 7:
Fold down the top half of the model, and crease. Your model should now look like this.

STEP 8:
Fold the model in half, crease hard, and unfold. Then fold down the right-hand side of the model so it lines up with the center crease you've just made.

Next, fold down the left-hand side of the model.

Now unfold the two folds you've just made, and your model should look like this.

STEP 9:

Finally, gently open out the model along the long, top edge so it forms a boat shape. The creases you made in Step 8 will allow you to flatten the base of the candleholder so it sits flat on a tabletop.

STEP 10:

Now make a second boat-shaped section and sit one inside the other. The candleholder is now complete.

STEP 11:

Make another eight candleholders, add your candles or LED tealights, and your lights are ready to be arranged to create a menorah.

Origami Baskets

These mini origami baskets are perfect for holding a small serving of Hanukkah treats, such as candy, fruit and nuts, or cookies. A sheet of origami paper that's 6 inches (15 cm) square will make a small basket that measures about 2 inches (5 cm) across.

To make a basket, you will need:

Two sheets of paper in your choice of blue, white, or silver

Glue   Scissors

STEP 1:

We chose to make a basket that's pale blue with dark blue patterns, so we began by placing the paper with the pale blue facing up.

Fold in half from side to side, crease, and then unfold. Fold in half from top to bottom, crease, and unfold.

STEP 2:

Turn the paper over. Fold in half from side to side, crease, and then unfold. Fold in half from top to bottom, crease, and unfold.

STEP 3:

Your piece of paper should now look like this.

Using the creases you made in steps 1 and 2, fold up the paper by bringing point A in to meet point B, and point C down to meet point D.

Collapse and flatten the model to form a square.

open points

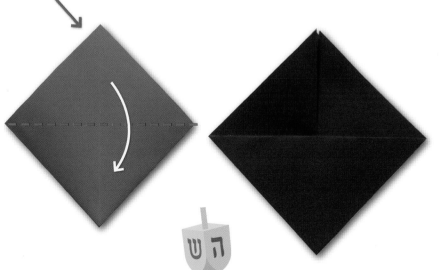

STEP 4:

Now turn the model 180 degrees so the open points are at the top. Then fold down the top layer of paper along the dotted line, and crease.

21

STEP 5:

Now fold the top layer of paper back up again so the bottom point meets the center of the model, and crease.

Then fold the top layer up one more time, and crease.

STEP 6:

Next, take hold of the right-hand point of the model, and working only with the top layer of paper, fold the right-hand side toward the left-hand side, just like turning the page of a book.

Then fold the point back toward the right-hand side so it meets the center of the model, and crease.

Now fold the section of the model you've been working with back toward the right-hand side—again, just like turning the page of a book.

Repeat everything in step 6 on the left-hand side of the model.

right-hand point

right-hand point

Fold this section back toward the right-hand side.

Your model should now look like this.

STEP 7:

Turn the model over and repeat steps 4 to 6. Your model should now look like this.

STEP 8:

Fold up the bottom of the model along the dotted line, crease hard, and unfold.

This part will pop open.

base of basket

bottom of basket

Now take hold of points A and B and gently pull them apart. The basket will start to pop open. Then you will carefully need to open out the base of the basket, flatten the bottom, and smooth out all the corners and edges.

base of basket

Your basket should now look like this.

STEP 9:

Fold down points A and B along the dotted lines, and tuck them neatly inside the basket. If you wish, you can glue them in place.

Points A and B are now in here.

STEP 10:

Finally, to make the basket's handle, cut a thick strip of paper from the second sheet. Fold it into three and glue the edge down.

handle

Slot the ends of the handle into the sides of the basket and glue them in place.

23

A Box for Gifts

Giving gifts is a special part of the Hanukkah celebrations. And what could be more special than a gift that's presented in a pretty origami box that's been made by you?

This next project shows you how to make a box with a lid. You can make mini boxes from squares of origami paper for small items such as jewelry or candy. Or make larger boxes from sheets of thick gift-wrapping paper. As long as you start with a square piece of paper, the design will work no matter the size of your paper.

Your friends and family will love receiving a Hanukkah gift in a handmade, **unique** gift box.

To make a box, you will need:

Two sheets of paper in your choice of colors (one sheet should be slightly smaller than the other)

STEP 1:

Place the paper colored side down. Fold in half from side to side, crease, and unfold. Fold in half from top to bottom, crease, and unfold.

STEP 2:

Now fold each of the four corners into the center of the model, and crease each edge well.

STEP 3:

Fold the top and the bottom of the model into the center, and crease hard.

25

STEP 4:

Unfold the top and bottom points of the model and smooth them flat.

STEP 5:

Now fold the sides of the model into the center, and crease well.

STEP 6:

Fold the top of the model toward the left-hand along the dotted line, crease well, and unfold. Then repeat on the other side.

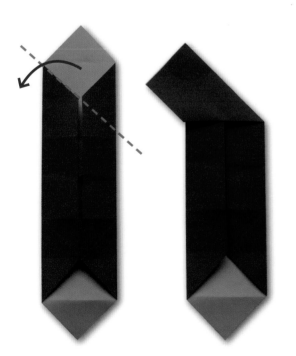

Then repeat this step on the bottom of the model.

A   B

STEP 7:

Now take hold of points A and B and gently open them out. As you do this, the top of the model will rise up.

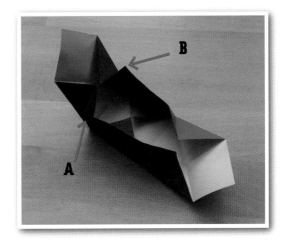

B

A

Fold the top point of the model inside the box and crease all the edges to shape the top edge of the box.

Repeat on the bottom of the model, and one half of your gift box is complete.

STEP 8:

Now take the second piece of paper and repeat all the steps to make the other half of the box.

The half of the box made with the bigger piece of paper will be the lid.

A Bow for Gifts

To complete your Hanukkah preparations, make some blue and white origami bows to decorate your gifts. You can make bows from origami paper or from recycled gift-wrapping paper.

You can even write a personal message in the center of your bow, to turn it into a bow and gift tag all in one. Have fun folding!

To make the origami bow, you will need:

Pen

One sheet of paper in your
choice of color

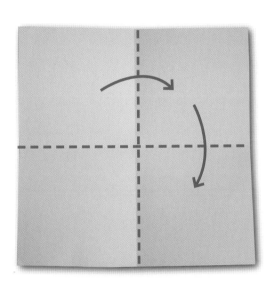

STEP 1:
Place the paper colored side down.
Fold in half from side to side,
crease, and unfold. Fold in half from
top to bottom, crease, and unfold.

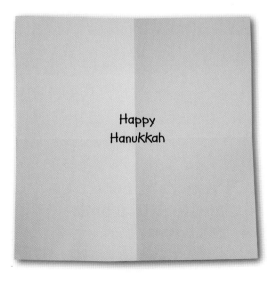

Happy
Hanukkah

STEP 2:
In the center of the paper
write a short Hanukkah
message. The message can
only fill about 1 square
inch (2.5 sq cm) of paper.

STEP 3:
Now fold the four corners of the paper into the center and crease.

STEP 4:
Fold the four corners into the center of the model again, and crease well.

STEP 5:
Now fold the model's four corners into the center for a final time. The paper will be very thick, so crease hard.

STEP 6:

Fold the four top flaps of the model back along the dotted lines, and crease well.

STEP 7:

Now fold the next four flaps that are inside the model back on themselves, and crease.

Happy Hanukkah

STEP 8:

Finally, fold the last four flaps in the center of the model back on themselves, and crease. Your message will now be revealed!

Glossary

emblem
A symbol used by a person or group of people as a means of identification.

miracle
An unexpected and favorable event that is not easily explained by science and that some may consider to be the work of a supreme being.

origami
The art of folding paper into decorative shapes or objects.

sculptures
Works of art that have a shape to them, such as statues or carved objects, and may be made of wood, stone, metal, plaster, or even paper.

symbol
Something that stands for or represents another thing, such as an important event or person. For example, a Star of David is a symbol of Judaism.

unique
One of a kind.

Index

C
candles, 4–5, 16

F
Festival of Lights, 16

G
gift bow origami model, 28–29, 30–31
gift box origami model, 24–25, 26–27
gifts, 4, 7, 24, 28

H
holiday wreath origami model, 12–13, 14–15

J
Japan, 4

M
menorahs 16

O
origami baskets, 20–21, 22–23
origami (general), 4, 6–7

S
simple origami menorah model, 16–17, 18–19
Star of David, 7, 8
Star of David origami model, 8–9, 10–11

Websites

www.activityvillage.co.uk/make-a-dreidel
www.chabad.org/kids/article_cdo/aid/354748/jewish/Chanukah.htm
www.thesprucecrafts.com/kids-crafts-to-celebrate-hanukkah-4117938

TITLES IN THIS SERIES

LET'S CELEBRATE WITH MORE CHRISTMAS ORIGAMI

LET'S CELEBRATE WITH MORE HALLOWEEN ORIGAMI

LET'S CELEBRATE WITH MORE HANUKKAH ORIGAMI

LET'S CELEBRATE WITH MORE THANKSGIVING ORIGAMI

LET'S CELEBRATE WITH MORE VALENTINE'S DAY ORIGAMI

LET'S CELEBRATE WITH ST. PATRICK'S DAY ORIGAMI

ISBN: 9781978526631
6-pack ISBN: 9781978526648

9 781978 526631

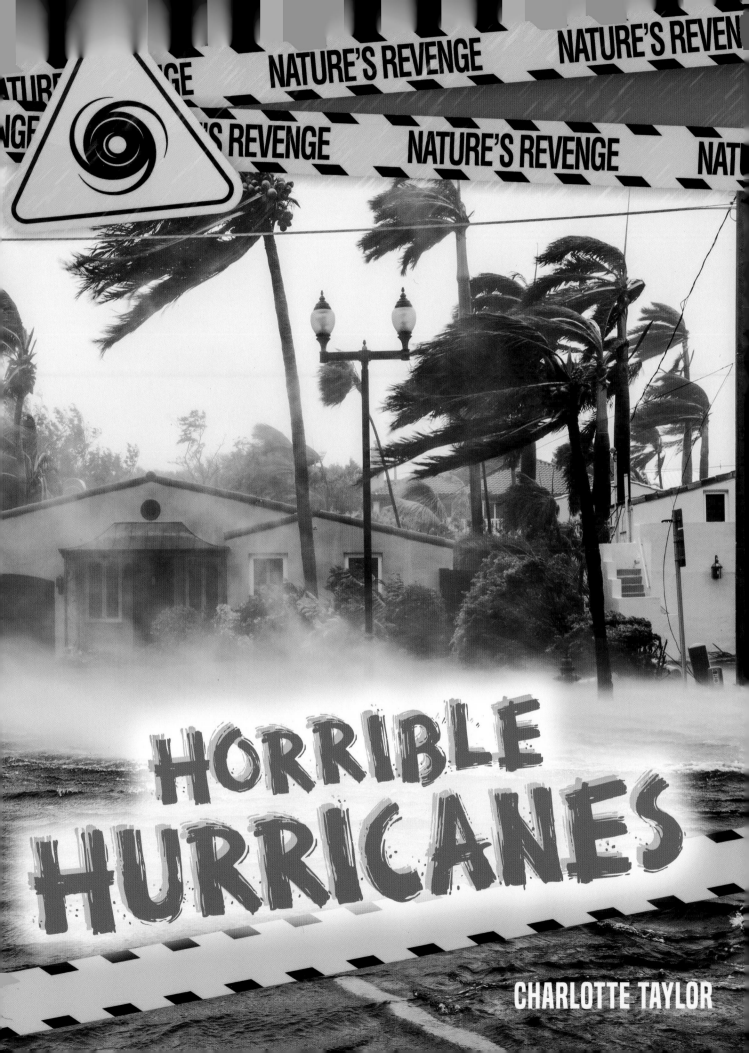

HORRIBLE HURRICANES

CHARLOTTE TAYLOR